C O P I N G
W I T H
H E L E N
L E D E R E R

Coping with Helen Lederer

HOW TO GET
THE BETTER
OF LIFE

*Helen Lederer, Roger Planer
and Richard McBrien*

ANGUS
& ROBERTSON
PUBLISHERS

ANGUS & ROBERTSON PUBLISHERS

16 Golden Square, London W1R 4BN,
United Kingdom, and Unit 4, Eden Park,
31 Waterloo Road, North Ryde, NSW, Australia 2113

First published in the United Kingdom by
Angus & Robertson (UK) in 1988

Copyright © Helen Lederer, Roger Planer, Richard McBrien 1988
Photographs © Stephen Hyde 1988

British Library Cataloguing in Publication Data
Lederer, Helen
  Coping with Helen Lederer: how to get the
  better of life.
  I. Title
  828'.91407

ISBN 0 207 16091 0

Typeset in Palatino by AKM Associates (UK) Ltd,
Ajmal House, Hayes Road, Southall, London
Printed in Great Britain by
Richard Clay Ltd, Chichester, Sussex

Front and back cover photographs by Stephen Hyde
Inside photographs by Stephen Hyde and John Ward

A NOTE FROM HELEN LEDERER'S AGENT

Since she was born Helen has quickly become a major figure in her own right. In a relatively short space of time she has got to the top of her tree with flying colours and has been impressing men and women alike as a name to watch out for.

The daughter of her father, she soon delighted all with her infectious abilities, the least of which have been noted by all. She was soon spotted and went on to build a reputation for herself which didn't go unnoticed. She now looks set to break through to even greater things in the future. Her many accomplishments are numbered and she has been described in some of the leading journals of the day.

You'll certainly be hearing more of Helen Lederer in the not too distant future, and what's more the future is looking very rosy indeed for this small fat show-off.

CONTENTS

Coping with:

ASSERTIVENESS

Much of my early life was plagued by an inability to say no. As a child my sister derived great satisfaction from the simple pleasure of driving over my foot in her transit van. A kind and protective soul, she would always ask my permission first. I hadn't the heart to tell her the bones in my foot were severely fractured and there was a danger I might never be able to walk again. I simply could not say no.

Learning to Say No

The desire to please and the reluctance to cause embarrassment are admirable qualities in themselves but they must be kept in proportion. Once, after a party, a couple mistook me for a mini-cab driver. I was too embarrassed to tell them they were wrong and ended up driving them all the way to Epsom.

If the problem of saying 'no' to other people seems insurmountable, start off by saying it to yourself. Try denying yourself something you would really quite like. For example:

> *Helen:* I would really like a bath.
> *Helen:* No.
> *Helen:* Please can I have a bath?
> *Helen:* No.
> *Helen:* But it's been three weeks now and
> I'm really very smelly.
> *Helen:* No.

Just as it is important to say 'no' it is also important not to take 'no' as an answer. This conversation can therefore continue for several hours:

Helen: No.
Helen: No.
Helen: No.
Helen: No.

As you grow more confident you can try your new skill on strangers. I spent several weeks walking up to complete strangers and simply saying 'No!' Very few challenged me on this, in fact I think they respected me for it.

You can now try it on something more difficult, for instance when a waiter asks you to pay the bill.

> *Waiter:* **Please will you pay the bill?**
> *Helen:* No.
> *Waiter:* **Get out of here and never come back!**
> *Helen:* No.

Sometimes even when you are saying 'no' your face is saying 'yes' – this can be confusing.

If there is any doubt I use my No face:

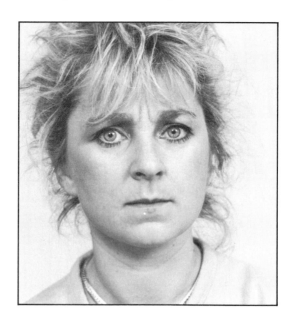

Overcoming Shyness

Part of learning to be assertive is overcoming our natural reluctance to mix with other people. Shyness can seriously inhibit your relationships with other people. Some of my relationships have been so badly inhibited by shyness that I haven't even had them.

To overcome shyness, wrinkle your nose at somebody on a train or bus. This may not sound like much, but it is the first stage in the lengthy process of breaking down the barriers between ourselves and the outside world. At first, a nod or a squint may be the only response you will get. But soon you will be rewarded by twitches, winks and flared nostrils. The whole compartment will be vibrating with non-verbal communication.

You should also make more of an effort to talk to people. If you see someone digging up the road take the time to go over and tell them how well you think they are doing it. I have had several interesting conversations in this way.

If an office colleague crosses you at work and you feel a particular need to assert yourself, try ransoming their personal coffee mug. Leave a note suggesting that their mug will be smashed unless they comply with your demands. Office rituals run deep, and this threat will put them at your mercy.

BODY LANGUAGE

People say more with their bodies than they ever do in conversation. Their movements and gestures are signals, instructing us on how they feel and how we ought to behave. That is why it is vital that we are able to interpret body language correctly.

Here is a candid photo of a recent dinner party of mine to illustrate some typical body language.

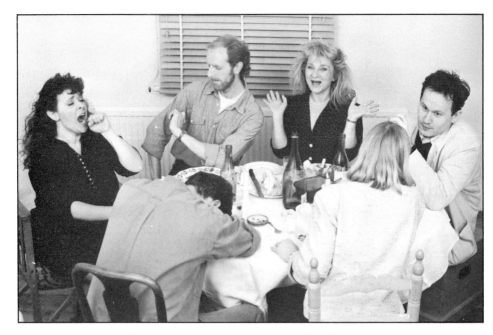

Here are some friends transfixed by me

This man is obviously hoping the other guests will go soon so that he can have me to himself

A guest trying to work out how, even at this late hour, I manage to remain enchanting, elegant, radiant, witty and effervescent

This woman has noticed a leak in the ceiling, but is so anxious not to embarrass me that she is preparing to catch the drip in her mouth

*This man is plucking up the courage
to ask me for the recipe*

*'That's odd that everyone should have a
baby-sitter to get back for at nine o'clock'*

14

GETTING HEALTHY

Every now and then you may be overcome by a strong desire to 'get fit'. Don't worry, this happens to most people once or twice a year. Although this feeling will soon go away of its own accord, it is important to know how to address yourself to it when it arrives.

Your 'health kick' has probably been inspired by one or other of the following:

A sunny day

A prolonged examination in front of the mirror

A long 'resting period' inbetween relationships which is becoming worrying

A reaction to a night of excessive indulgence

An impending meeting with an important employer or potential lover

The minute you feel your health kick coming on it is vital that you decide which of the above has triggered it off. It may not be necessary for you to do anything too drastic. A sunny day, for instance, can easily be counteracted by a filthy depression and you can redress the balance of a particularly drunken evening with a few pine kernels from a health food shop. However, in serious cases you will have no choice but to go to a health club.

Going to a Health Club

Your membership will have lapsed since your last attempted health kick. Adjust the expiry date.

As you climb the steps to the club you will probably get a little out of breath. To save yourself embarrassment, pause before entering the reception area. You are then ready to apologise to the receptionist for not having been in for a while. Say something like: 'Sorry, been a bit busy recently – been away – on a charity walk.' You can now enter the changing rooms without guilt.

The Changing Room

Changing rooms in health clubs provide an opportunity for people of the same sex to wander around freely with very few clothes on and pretend not to be interested in each others' bits. There is an art to appearing truly uninterested which only seasoned health fanatics have mastered.

On entering you will notice a number of people preparing to have a shower. Thin people will be wearing small towels which regularly fall off as if by mistake. Fat people will be wrapped up in enormous towels and will appear to have great difficulty with their locker door until all the thin people have left. They will then shed their towels and walk backwards into the shower, their bottoms against a wall.

None of this will alarm you until you realise that you have forgotten to put your bathing costume on underneath your clothes. Only carefully planned disrobing will save you from embarrassment.

In the Swimming Pool

Once you have changed you will see a lot of people in goggles and nose clips swimming relentlessly up and down the length of the pool. Don't let this put you off. If half way through your first width you bump into one of them, use this as an opportunity to catch your breath and have a little chat. You may find it necessary to explain that you have been very busy recently and consequently your swimming has had to take second place to more important intellectual pursuits.

Safety

A swimming pool can be a dangerous place and we all have to take responsibility for each other. Finding that your costume has disappeared up your bot, revealing one if not both buttocks can be mortifying. If you see someone to whom this has happened it is your *responsibility* to tell the attendant *at once*. For safety's sake act immediately, they'll thank you for it later.

Coming off Your Health Kick

Your health kick will die naturally in a matter of days, or weeks at most. There are, however, a number of things you can do to hurry it along:

> **Not finding the time. By juggling with your working schedule and bringing a few appointments forward you can easily make regular exercise impossible to fit in**

> **Buying a second-hand tennis racket from an Oxfam shop that snaps can prove a useful setback to your excercise programme**

> **A good long look in the mirror after a workout. You may see a new you, or you may see a bloated wreck with a red and blotchy face panting with exhaustion**

A PAGE FROM MY PERSONAL RECIPE BOOK

It's just this sort of photograph that leaves many aspiring cooks feeling depressed and inadequate. How can one possibly produce something that looks as good as this? The problem with most recipe books is that they don't anticipate the practical difficulties experienced by would-be cooks. Here is a tried and tested favourite of mine that I have adapted over the years.

I have called this recipe 'Lederer's Layered Lasagne' but don't worry if what you end up with is a chicken casserole – when I first made this one it was meant to be 'Beef Julienne'. Treat it very much as a movable feast.

Layered Lasagne

INGREDIENTS

Lasagne
Leeks
Mushrooms
Onions
Chervil leaves
Yoghurt
Strong cheddar cheese
Beaten egg
Legumes

1. Thoroughly mix eggs.

2. Place layers of lasagne in pan of boiling water.

3. Boil the leeks and then set them aside.

4. Put the mushrooms in a pan and form a roux.

5. Finely chop and mix in your chervil leaves.

6. Mix the mushrooms and onions in with some live yoghurt.

7. Season to taste.

8. Take the lasagne out of the boiling water, and place layers in a flame-proof dish, spreading the mixture between the lasagne. Bake in oven until browned.

Book a cab now, before you start, because in ten minutes time you will realise that you have forgotten a vital ingredient. The timing in most recipes is always unrealistic. Also, allow ten minutes to find the eggs.

What for? Seems like a terrible waste of leeks. Leave this one out.

I don't think you can form a roux on your own. I think you might need friends. If you're cooking alone you'd best leave this one out and get on to the next stage.

Don't panic if you've never even heard of chervil leaves. Nor have I. Look around for a substitute. I sacrificed my yucca plant. It wasn't looking well anyway.

5b. Marinate in alcohol. This instruction does not actually belong in this recipe. It is however one of my favourite ones. Thoroughly saturate yourself in alcohol before attempting the next stage.

I was thoroughly put off this when I discovered what live yoghurt meant. Leave this out unless you like the idea of having lots of little yoghurt germs giving birth on your tongue.

On the back of a bottle of tabasco it said "guaranteed to enhance any meal", so I usually put some of that in.

I really would advise this – I have learnt from experience that serving it in the boiling water can be disastrous.

19

Tips on Serving

Creating the correct ambience is very important. Atmospheric lighting not only makes the evening special but helps disguise burnt or charred food.

Plates of course should be warmed. Don't worry if you haven't got a plate warmer, wrap them up in a woolly scarf.

Creative Timing

If, like me, you find that everything is not ready in time simply explain to your guests that it is now very chic to serve meals in 'nouvelle ordre'. This consists of serving the peas and chocolate sauce for a starter, followed by cheese and biscuits, then the sweet, coffee and after-dinner mints, concluding with the main course.

Plates of course should be warmed.
If you haven't got a plate warmer,
wrap them up in a woolly scarf

EATING OUT

Going out for a meal can be a daunting experience, but with a bit of planning can be as agreeable as eating in. There's nothing stopping you from carrying a few spare crudités in your bag in case there is some particularly nice sauce to finish up.

Eating on your own or with another woman may considerably confuse a waiter. He may be forced to go to another table to find a man to taste the wine. Or if there are no other men in the restaurant he may have to pick someone off the street.

Or he may repeatedly ignore your attempts to catch his attention making you feel uncharismatic and ineffectual in the eyes of everyone else in the restaurant. Yet if you are being particularly intimate with your partner, he may well pick this moment to bring you some extra vegetables that you didn't order.

PARTIES

Given the right preparation and the necessary relaxed attitude there is no reason why your parties shouldn't be as successful as mine. All you need to do is pay attention to details, such as inviting people, buying drink and remembering to be in on the night. Getting the right mix and number of people is vital. You cannot always assume that everyone you invite will turn up – I usually allow for a 90 per cent drop-out rate. A correctly worded, pleasantly set-out invitation is likely to increase your chances:

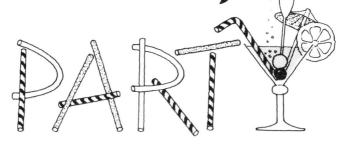

Helen invites you to a

PART

8.00 *Saturday November 10th*

Bring a bottle

Please come to my party (but only if you want to). I promise the drink won't run out this time and there won't be any of that paella that seemed to repeat rather unpleasantly throughout the evening. And there will be other people there.

So please come on the 10th if you can make it; if you can't, it'll be on the 19th, or possibly the 27th if that will be more convenient, or maybe you think I shouldn't have one at all which is fine, just let me know and I'll cancel the whole thing.

Oh, and if you're the person who threw up on the sofa perhaps you'd like to eat before you arrive this time (the cushions came up very well considering).

R.S.P.C.A.

```
Please fill in this questionnaire for future reference - if it's not
too much trouble - so I know whether to bother inviting you again, ever.

1.  Do you like me?
                    a) a lot
                    b) a bit
                    c) indifferent
                    d) not at all?

2.  Did you find my last party
                    a) fab
                    b) amazing
                    c) challenging
                    d) other?

3.  Did you find my banana joke
                        a) hilarious
                        b) offensive
                        c) radically altered your perception
                           of the fruit/man debate?

4.  Did you think the fight
                        a) brought people together
                        b) was my fault for mentioning Peter's impotence
                        c) encouraged people to go home a bit early?

            Please do not defecate this form
```

Preparing the Ground

You may feel reluctant to hold a party because you are
frightened of what people will think of your home. I know
just how you feel – guests tend to make snap judgements
which can take months of persuasion to dispel. An old gonk
found underneath a cushion can ruin your credibility and
destroy your confidence for the whole evening.

By paying attention to details you can guarantee to
create the right impression. I know before I entertain I take
time to prepare the ground. A noticeboard full of invitations,
a forged love letter peeping out of a book, a few present tags
left discreetly around the room, with messages such as 'hope
this diamond doesn't offend you', can considerably improve
your status.

Lighting can transform an ordinary flat. If your home is really ugly try turning out all the lights. You can always highlight plus features – most of my parties are spent in virtual darkness.

Stains on the carpet can be a worry. A succession of spillages from casually eaten meals has left my carpet badly stained. However, with a little imagination and creative furniture management this needn't be immediately obvious. Simply edge sofas, chairs and tables over the offending marks.

If anyone should comment on your strange posture introduce the idea as a game along the lines of Twister Fun.

Being the Perfect Hostess

Many people arrive at a party or social gathering highly apprehensive about the prospect of having to talk to complete strangers. I always spot these people, take them aside and give detailed instructions on what they should and shouldn't say about politics and current affairs.

Sometimes things still go wrong. Nervous blinking, profuse nodding and appealing looks to other guests are all signs that someone needs to be rescued. I have been known to leave people in this condition if they haven't brought a bottle.

Games

Some guests shy away from games feeling that they are competitive and potentially humiliating, and indeed they can reveal things about your friends you never realised were true. Simply announce that it is time for games, and if anyone protests reassure them that it is only 'harmless fun' even though you know this to be untrue.

Some of my old favourites include: 'When was the Last Time you were Unfaithful?', 'Spot the Illiterate' and 'Who's the Least Intelligent Person Here?'. It can be hilarious to find out just how little some people know on certain subjects. The person who knows least about anything has to do the washing-up or leave early as a forfeit.

If people don't like formalised games, why not try talking about someone behind their back then tell them and see if they can guess what you said?

DANCE

The way people dance is as different as their signatures. My own dance style is a free expression of how I am feeling at that moment and is unhindered by rhythm or indeed music. I call it my 'me as I am' dance and I must say quite a few people have commented on it over the years.

So practised am I at communicating through movement, that I now find I have to moderate my dance in public because perfect strangers were beginning to deduce the intimate details of my private life. I now reserve my 'full' dance for friends and loved ones at home.

If I find a special person who I wish would know me better, I often perform my 'life history dance'. The extracts you can see here will demonstrate just how extraordinarily revealing this dance can be.

As you can see, my partner is preparing himself
for the re-enactment of my Maths 'O'-level

Here he is having to restrain himself as I've
touched him deeply with my story

HOLDING YOUR OWN IN CONVERSATION

There are few things I enjoy more than having a cultured conversation with a really well-informed person. It gives me an opportunity to say things like 'empirical', 'Nosferatu' and 'really evocative'. It's not always necessary to stick to the point, the art here is to make the person you are talking to feel as uncertain as you are about what it is you are both talking about.

There are, however, some subjects on which I have become embarrassingly unstuck in the past. There is no need for this to happen to you. I have outlined some popular confusions here in a brief guide.

Cultural Guide

Backgammon – *board game*
Gammon steak – *a cut of meat*

Brandenburg – *concerto*
Battenburg – *a cake (the boxes can look similar)*

Degas – *always dancers*

NF/NFT – *an easy confusion. Don't expect to*

find a Hungarian film at an NF rally

Pigeon filo envelope – *nothing to do with diaries, messages or personal organisers*

Pointilism – *painting by numbers*

Renoir – *puffy women who don't appear to mind about it much*

Seurat – *a French pointilist*
Sewer rat – *someone I went out with in 1987*

Improving Your Discourse

The secret of a successful exchange is to nod enthusiastically and then disagree. Always ask the person to be 'more specific' or 'less specific'. If someone puts across a particularly good point suggest that they might be being 'dogmatic' or 'simplistic'. Only ever agree 'in some respects', never whole-heartedly. If all else fails simply say: 'It's all relative anyway'.

Dinner-Table Conversation

Here is an example of a typical cultural exchange at a restaurant with some of my friends after we'd been to see a Fassbinder film. As you can see I have not allowed myself to be intimidated and nor should you.

Daniel: That was an excellent seafood salad.
Clare: Didn't you think that his direction was too densely analagous?
Helen: No, I thought it was delicious . . . in an empirical sense.
Daniel: I must remember to ask whether the mangetouts were individually blanched. I've been worrying about it all evening.
Helen: Yes, I think they were — hypothetically speaking.
Clare: I thought the visuals overtook the

content, alienating people into a
common form of ignorance and
apathy.

Helen: Yes, I agree. Nosferatu . . .

Daniel: Do you like zucchini, Helen?

Helen: Some of his early work is good. I
don't like his use of dialogue though.

Clare: It's wonderfully crisp.

Helen: It's all relative anyway.

T R A F F I C   J A M S

There are many positive things to be gained from finding
yourself in a traffic jam – once you accept that getting to your
destination is not one of them. Here is a great opportunity to
get out and meet people. There are potential acquaintances in
their tens and twenties who have no alternative but to
receive your overtures of friendship. I've been known to keep
in touch with people that I've met in a traffic jam for years. I
have even caused a few traffic jams myself when re-
encountering them.

> *Remember: the red light doesn't necessarily mean stop.*

STREET CRED

Being in does not mean staying inside your house, it means being stylish and on the ball – having street credibility.

'Street cred' is something you either have or haven't got. Apparently I do not have it but I am prepared to acquire some if someone will tell me where to get it and what it is.

As far as I can gather you can get cred by waiting near bus stops or in front of some graffiti. Here is a picture of me at a particularly cred place which took me some hours to find in the car.

COPING
WITH MEN

Here is a picture of a man I know, on holiday in Greece. His name is Steve. For some reason he is about to pour Retsina into his trousers.

Things Not to Do with Men

Do not go on holiday with them to Greece. Two weeks in Crete on the cusp of the rainy season is particularly inadvisable.

Do not entrust them with your soggy espadrilles, they may think it is funny to skewer them on a kebab stick and roast them on a barbeque.

Men Do Care

Contrary to popular opinion, men do care. They are very sensitive on certain subjects. Here is a picture of a Steve after I had suggested that the Dolby system on his ghetto blaster was possibly not as good as that on a conventional hi-fi.

Complexes

Men's sense of security can easily be shaken. I found that by affectionately calling one man 'Tom Thumb' I was inadvertently reinforcing a complex he had about his size.

Speech

Although men are capable of speech, on the whole they tend not to use this facility. However, when pressed some men will respond with something along the following lines:

> 'You don't want to get involved with a man like me' – when men say this they mean you do want to get involved with a man like me who is deeply challenging and interesting beneath this surly exterior. The best response to this is: 'You're right, I don't want to get involved with a man like you.'

> 'Is it time for Newsnight yet?' – this is very positive. It means that he's going to stick with you at least until the end of the programme.

Letters

Letters can be even more difficult than speech to interpret:

> Dear Helen,
> This is a very difficult letter to write. I feel I must tell you that I can only give you so much rope before the foundations begin to crumble. The other night I thought that the thread might snap and everything we've tried to build together would erupt into thin air. But I really believe if we unravelled the threads we could in time do so. I hope you understand, because sometimes it's really difficult to say these

things face to face, but when you write them down everything's so much clearer, isn't it?

Yours faithfully (except for that once)

It is impossible to take an objective view of such a letter, you are far too emotionally involved to be able to stand back and read it correctly. Indeed, even your friends will be too involved to help. I find it best to read it out to complete strangers and ask their opinion. Waiters, taxi drivers and bank clerks are particularly sympathetic and can offer lasting advice.

In the above case I decided, after much consultation and consideration, to send a written reply:

Dear ——

Two main things: one, you smell and two, it's over.

Yours sincerely,

Helen

Making Men Sensitive

In my relationships, I feel it's important that a man should be able to cry without shame. I have often been known to hit men repeatedly about the head just to help them towards this experience. I then say reassuring things like 'Don't worry, let it all out – it's good to cry'.

Men are often reluctant to talk about their emotions but by employing the latest breakthroughs in behavioural psychology you can get them to open up. Use rewards and punishments to encourage emotional honesty – for example, offer him a bar of chocolate and then refuse to give it to him until he tells you how vulnerable he feels.

Living with Men

I have found that moving into a flat with a man is a very good way of making him suddenly realise how important it is for you to maintain your independence. They might, for instance, say things like:

> 'When I said I loved you, I meant yes I love you being here, but I might appreciate you even more if you were somewhere else'.

This can be very frustrating especially when he invited you there in the first place and you voluntarily gave up a perfectly good flat to move in to a small, grimy hovel out of your own choice. Still, it is all part of a learning experience.

Avoiding Men

Sometimes it is necessary to avoid persistent men. I find a brief note usually does the trick:

> Dear ——
>
> Due to a sprained ankle, I am afraid Helen Lederer cannot attend the cinema this evening. Unfortunately this also means she cannot answer the phone.
>
> Signed by,
>
> (Helen's mother)

THE FIRST DATE

When you go on a first date there are certain things you should take:

Passport   Pens, paper, envelopes
Multilingual phrasebook   Insulating tape
Sponge bag   Books
Fruit   Trowel
Mirror   Dressing-gown
Maps/atlas   Toothbrush
Travellers cheques   Change of clothes
Crash helmet

Here is a photo of me on a first date:

If your date cannot tolerate the idea of a well-prepared woman then he is probably not worth knowing anyway

My ideal date is:
Someone who doesn't go to the toilet in the basin.

SEDUCTION

Preparation

If you're like me when you go to other people's houses you can't resist browsing in bathroom cabinets, reading old letters, bank statements, listening to answering machines and photocopying personal documents – all just healthy inquisitiveness. So before I invite someone into my home I take certain precautions. I gather up all my bathroom accessories, all the creams, ointments and pills, pop them in a plastic bag and hang them out of the window. As the relationship develops and I feel more secure I gradually reintroduce things back into the bathroom cupboard.

There is nothing certain men like more than mending something – it instantly engages them and increases their confidence. So just before my date arrives I sometimes break something. It's a small price to pay to put him at his ease – but do keep it simple. Before one potential partner arrived I pulled out several feet of copper pipes from my boiler. Sadly, he was unable to reconnect the heating, or stem the flood which turned out to be the most pressing concern of the evening. So use your common sense – take height and strength into account – a small man should be given an appropriate task such as hoovering the carpet with his mouth.

Strategies

For a really successful seduction your lover should think that he is seducing you. This is not as easy as it may sound, especially if he is trying to leave at the time. However, there is one successful strategy which my mother passed on to me.

The Valance

At the end of a pleasant evening, casually introduce the subject of beds and bedrooms into the conversation. Obviously you cannot tackle this head-on, it needs to be within, say, the context of bedroom furnishings as a whole. You can then say something like: 'Would you like to look at my valance before you go home?' The right man will instantly know not only that a valance is a frill that goes round a bed but will take the hint and go into the bedroom.

Man: I like a well-dressed bed

*Helen: Do you think the colour
          is all right?*
*Man: Oh yes, a good valance
          should complement the
          undersheet and contrast
          with the duvet.*

*Helen: But don't you think pleats
          would have been nice?*
*Man: Pleats are easily scuffed
          which can be tough
          on cleaning bills*

Helen: I'm glad you mentioned
that because I have several
valances from my
grandmother that I
simply don't dare use.
Man: Oh?

Man: This one is particularly
exquisite.
Helen: I know

*The evening was a great success. Together we
planned a trip to Bentalls sale the very next day.
We rushed happily through the linen
department, from one display case to the next
and picked up many a bargain along the way. So
really, things couldn't have worked out better*

Afterwards

The morning after can be even more traumatic than the
night before. It is not so much the decision as to whether or
not you wish to see the person again, but how best to let him
know. After years of being misunderstood – I once lost the
best lover of my life by asking him if he wanted a lift home – I
have hit on some simple phrases which seem to do the trick.

If you do not wish to see him again casually let drop
remarks such as: 'I never sleep with someone unless I'm really
serious' or 'I want to beget a child with you'.

SEX

A lot of nonsense has been talked about sex ever since it was discovered in 1964. Consequently, many of us go through life feeling desperately ashamed of our sexual feelings, fearing that we will be shunned and despised if we own up to them.

But the good news about sex nowadays is that whatever you want to do, it's all right – so long as you've discussed it first with your partner, or partners, or with yourself if you're on your own.

You may want regular, three-times-a-week sex (but don't worry if it's less than that or more). Or you may have a secret desire to have sex in an unusual place like a phone box or a bus queue. This is nothing to worry about – unless you like worrying about it which is perfectly all right as well. All these things are all right, so long as you've discussed them with whoever you want to do it with, whether it be a man, a woman or a kebab. I should know, I always discuss it first, afterwards and during it as well.

Having an Affair

You may be deeply in love with someone and not even considering having an affair, but it is just as well to discuss the possibility. It's a good idea to phone round any friends who you think you might conceivably have an affair with to discuss it in case the impulse takes you at a later date. It would be a shame to ruin the spontaneity of the moment should the occasion arise.

COPING WITH CRITICISM

A hurtful remark can hang over you for weeks, loading you down with nagging fears and self doubts. How do you know whether to take someone's criticism of you seriously? Could it be that they have a problem which they are projecting onto you?

I am my own severest critic and it is rare for anyone to come up with an observation on my behaviour that I wasn't already aware of myself. I have made a list of my own faults which I put under my magnetic ladybird on my fridge door. If someone criticises me and the fault is not on the list then they are wrong. Here is my list which I blushingly acknowledge.

MY FAULTS

I am too generous

I am too kind

I bite my toenails

I am quite prepared to discuss these flaws with anyone observant enough to have noticed them. Indeed, I am more than happy to discuss them over a meal provided the conversation doesn't stray back to my critic's problems.

F R I E N D S

It may be that when you visit a friend they are not standing at the door welcoming you with the smell of freshly baked bread wafting from the oven and a large chocolate cake on the table with Welcome written in pink icing. It may not be that they have managed to buy tickets for you to see a special film or donated a nice jumper that they no longer wear. This can be disappointing.

However, if you expect less of people you won't be so devastated. You may even become grateful and pleased that they are in at all when you call to see them. Just thank them for the little things. Your greeting of, 'Hey, you're in, what a delight' will sound more friendly and be more useful than, 'So where's the chocolate cake then?'

Normality

In any case, according to Desmond Morris all human beings have the capacity to experience only 2.6 friends. Obviously you may be concerned if your total reaches 3.6 as mine did at one point in my life. I simply sent one friend to Coventry, bringing it down to 3, and was a bit offhand to another which gave me the necessary half-friend/half-acquaintance category, meeting the .6 target.

ELEMENTARY PHYSICS AND THE HUMAN CONDITION

During my research days in the lab (Monday and Friday afternoons, Blackheath High School for Girls) we carried out a very useful experiment in hydraulics. The basic empirical basis of this theorem is, to put it in a nutshell, without going into a lot of complicated scientific vernacular that the reader might not understand, that if you put a lot of pressure on something inside a container, eventually the lid will blow off.

How like life in all its many facets this is. For instance, you may find that a companion walks in a way which irritates you. Instead of saying nothing and letting the pressure build up inside you, confront your friend and explain that unless he changes the way he walks, your head may blow off. If questioned, refer him to 'Helen's Hydraulic Theorem'.

FIGHTING JEALOUSY

If you allow jealousy into your life it will grow into an overriding obsession. Your judgement and common sense will soon be swallowed up as they were for Othello, when he discovered Iago's sock in Desdemona's bed.

To the jealous person a single, seemingly innocent item can take on the most sinister meaning. For instance, if a person found a moon-shaped earring in his or her partner's bed, they might just feel a bit devastated by the fact that their partner could possibly be attracted by someone with absolutely no taste whatsoever. They might be forced to ask themselves the question, what sort of a person wears an earring with manky clips and fake rubies set into it?

If this happens, do as I did – do not lose your sense of perspective. Find a brick and throw it through his window.

Some experts in the field of human psychology have disagreed with me on this. A Freudian psychoanalyst whose advice I sought suggested instead that I break his knuckles with a mallet, whereas a Jungian therapist preferred the idea of strangulation with a dressing-gown cord.

The only problem with this sort of advice is that you might discover, as I did, that the earring was in fact your own. This can leave you with a good deal of explaining to do and possibly cast some doubt on your own taste in jewellery. But at least you have demonstrated that you care enough to be upset.

Some Further Suggestions

1. Show your partner you genuinely care for them. Make them a cup of tea in the morning, run their bath for them, or even hide in your car at night in a cul de sac under a tartan rug to keep careful watch over them. A mere flash of your headlights will let them know you're there, and confirm that bond of trust between you.

2. Lie awake at night and try to imagine your future partner. Think what they might be doing now and with whom? If he/she is incapable of being faithful to you now, what hope is there for your relationship in the future? Make sure you have serious words with them about this when you meet.

3. Go to a jealousy workshop and try to cure your obsession with your partner's fidelity. Better still, get your partner to go to one. This will give you a good opportunity to meet someone else.

SELF DEFENCE

I have developed my own method of Self Defence, taking the best from both Eastern and Western traditions and welding them into a practical, easy-to-learn technique which protects the body and enhances the soul.

Concentrate on the innermost core of your being. Centre yourself

Rock gently on your heels, repeat the sacred mantra 'Omm'

Hit him in the private area

HOW TO COPE IN THE RARE EVENT OF PEOPLE NOT LIKING YOU VERY MUCH

You may find it hard to believe, but there have been one or two people in my life whom I have simply failed to befriend. My offers of love and laughter have bounced off them like rain off a slate.

I sometimes have nightmares about all the fun that people are having without me. A discarded party seven or a frozen pea packet peeping out of a dustbin bag is enough to send me into a decline for several days.

If I see a lost kitten notice nailed to a tree I sometimes put one up of my own. Why should someone else have lost a kitten and not me?

And why is it that at certain kinds of dinner parties people always run out of individual pudding dishes when it comes to me? I often end up eating chocolate mousse out of a tea cup or even the bowl it was made in. And when it comes to coffee, purely by chance I'm given the mug with the china dog turd at the bottom.

Some Words of Comfort

On these occasions of loneliness and incomprehension I often take comfort from the tenets and proverbs learnt in my childhood. Blackheath High School for Girls instilled in me values and skills which have served me well throughout my life. It was there for instance that I learnt how to walk onto a rostrum with a straight back. An ability which went not a little way towards winning me the Elizabeth Garret prize for speech and spoken prose, at the age of twelve. (I keep a photocopy of the certificate in my purse should anyone show sufficient interest.)

I often recall that cheerful parable taught in an early scripture class when Our Lord encouraged a man to pick up his futon and walk – an image engraved on my mind. I like to return to it at moments of stress and find it to be a great comfort. I also remember the day I learnt to spell the word 'because' properly – but that's a different story.

INBETWEEN RELATIONSHIPS

If you find yourself sobbing uncontrollably on the tube, this could be a sign that you have just split up with your partner. Your friends' efforts to console you will do more harm than good. They will confess to you all the unpleasant things your ex-partner did behind your back. They will explain to you that they never liked him anyway – that they had sex with him and still didn't like him. You in turn will drive your friends mad by talking constantly of your ex-lover with a trembling lower lip.

> *Friend:* 'Nice day'
> *Helen:* 'Yes, Graham used to like the sun'
> *Friend:* 'Can't you shut up for just one second?'
> *Helen:* 'Yes, Graham used to say that . . .'

You will have to face the fact that you are no longer part of a unit and you must adjust to your new status. The state you are entering is called being 'Inbetween Relationships'. This basically means that someone has just dumped you and the next person is too frightened of your looks, beauty and talent to ask you out.

Analysing What Went Wrong

There is really no point in agonising over what went wrong. Remember, we choose our partners to redress any imbalance in ourselves. That is why I tend to pick people who are weak and spineless.

Loneliness

As you set out on your own, the wedding invitations will start to pile up on your mat. At these weddings you will meet more married people who will invite you to more weddings, where more married couples will remind you of your single status and your newfound popularity amongst married people.

Being on Your Own at Parties

Going to parties on your own will lead to inevitable disappointment, despite your hosts' good intentions. Their attempts to help you over this awkward situation can just make things worse:

> 'Angela and John, Clare and Michael meet Helen and empty chair. Helen and empty chair this is Angela and John and Clare and Michael. We were hoping that the incredibly interesting and handsome David would turn up tonight for Helen but unfortunately he is busy doing something incredibly interesting and handsome. Still, another time Helen. Anyway, I'm sure you and your empty chair will get along famously. You've got everything in common, except that the chair will still be standing at the end of the evening. Drinks anyone? Would your empty chair like anything else? A cushion perhaps. Helen's always gone for the strong silent type . . .'

Learning to Love Your Loneliness

Going out on your own in the hope of meeting someone requires enormous patience, and a good deal of reading material. Finding yourself without a newspaper in a pub or restaurant can mean resorting to reading the menu, the labels on your clothes, or the size of your shoes.

If you try to fight your loneliness, your loneliness will always win. Going out with others will only intensify your feeling of being alone, but if you stay at home and learn to appreciate it you will soon find that your loneliness has passed and before long you may even be mourning its loss.

Going to Dinner With Yourself

I frequently go to dinner with myself because I find my company stimulating. I serve myself a meal with all the trimmings: knives, forks and so on. I pour some of my favourite wine, because I know I like it – complain about it and then send it back. After a respectable amount of time spent on small talk, I begin to relax and feel thoroughly at home – because I am. I might then offer to help with the washing up and eventually one thing leads to another and I suggest going to bed – with myself. Obviously I have to face myself the following morning, but so long as no one gets hurt, I can live with it.

BEING DRUNK

'I drink therefore I'm fat'
Anon

Sometimes quite by accident you can find yourself danger-
ously drunk. It can happen to anyone and is very dis-
concerting if the situation you are in demands that you keep a
steady head.

How Did It Happen?

It most likely has something to do with what you have been
drinking. It may not be your fault. Misunderstanding an
advertising campaign might have resulted in you drinking
your way through several pints of 90° proof lager thinking it
was alcohol-free.

Nerves or absentmindedness may have played a part.
You may just have popped in for a packet of crisps and
absentmindedly consumed three flagons of scrumpy while
you were there. Or, out of politeness, you may have gone on
a three-day binge to comfort a friend.

What to Look Out for

When getting drunk your behaviour will go through various
stages which you should be aware of if you want to prevent
the situation getting out of hand. Swaying benignly is an
early warning sign, usually accompanied by the mistaken
conviction that everyone loves you. You may then start to

oscillate between aggressive bouts of fierce argument and outbursts of emotion when you tearfully reassure strangers that 'you're not always like this'.

When You've Had Enough

Three bottles of wine can easily mislead you as to the exact limit of your drinking capacity. A final cognac may just tip the balance, and everything you've drunk and eaten throughout the week may suddenly stir into action.

If you're out with someone you like, try to resist the temptation to invite them back for coffee, even though it may seem like a good idea at the time. If you have avoided being sick all over them in the restaurant there's still a good chance that you'll be sick all over your pillowcase. The next day you may find it difficult to reassure them that the chances of this happening again are very slight.

If you really enjoy drinking, it's much safer to do it on your own. There is no need to feel ashamed of being a secret drinker, though it's probably best not to include it as a hobby on your cv or mention it at job interviews. If you miss the camaraderie of social drinking it's not too hard to reconstruct the experience at home with a few of the right phrases.

> *Helen:* My shout, I think.
> *Helen:* No, I'll get them in.
> *Helen:* What are you having?
> *Helen:* Same again.
> *Helen:* Do you want a top-up?
> *Helen:* You've twisted my arm.
> *Helen:* How about one more for the road?
> *Helen:* All right, just a quick one then.

CRISIS

Few things are more traumatic than coping with a personal crisis. Imagine, for instance that you are trying to write a book on something you are supposed to know about and then something happens in your personal life and suddenly you lose confidence in your ability to write anything at all and then you start worrying about all the people who might buy that book assuming that you know all about how to cope seeing as you wrote it when in fact you might not actually be able to cope with everything completely all the time.

DEPRESSION

'Personal happiness is impossible. Four thousand years of civilisation and there has yet to be one truly happy human being. Love is a fantasy which turns cruelly upon itself, a cancer of the soul. The whole world is plunging inexorably towards mass destruction. People are selfish, vain and deceitful. All men have other girlfriends. Life is a hopeless compromise between misery and unhappiness.'

I have had these feelings myself and I know what it's like. Fears like this can eat you up. That's why it is important to *do* something *now*.

How to Overcome Depression

I have prepared a few dishes that I find are effective antidotes to depression.

Guacamole dip with croutons is a sure-fire way of dispelling fears about Armageddon, having your face torn off by shrapnel and radiation sickness

Pavlova with raspberry sauce reduces anxiety about South African repression of human rights, getting old and losing an earring

Rum truffles can deal with the really big issues such as a burst carrier bag and no messages on the answering machine.

59

Transference

Thinking about other people who are happy can be very depressing. Many people who are happily married with three children and a dog are only happy because they know how much they are depressing you. With people like this try saying how pleased you are about their happiness. This may well make them depressed and cheer you up.

CHEERING UP A PIECE OF FURNITURE

I took this rather dowdy chest of drawers I inherited and made it much more jolly.

The secret is to use a nice stencil – make your own. I made this very attractive flower on a rainy afternoon. You then simply spray through it with some colourful paint. Those big daisies make it look much more cheerful, don't they? I think if this chest could talk it would say thank you.

Rag rolling and marbling can lend any plain surface an elegant and sophisticated appearance, giving the humblest flat that envied classical look.

COPING WITH LONELINESS, BOREDOM AND THE SENSE OF BEING A VERY SMALL COG IN A LARGE MACHINE

Getting Involved in Your Community

One of the best ways to combat loneliness and boredom is to become involved in your local community. Perhaps there are too many bollards in your high street – or not enough bollards. There's nearly always something to get incensed about. If you're really stuck for ideas, why not dig up a few holes in the pavement and then see if you can sprain your ankle and sue the council for it?

A good place to start your community activities is with a visit to a car boot sale or post office queue. Mention a few local issues to like-minded people and invite them round for tea to talk about them. Make sure you pepper your conversation with expressions like 'people come first' and 'town planners must be mad' and you will soon become known as a 'community-minded person' or 'local activist'. As your new friends leave, casually inform them that they are now general secretary, treasurer or minute-taker.

Once you get established you can have a lot of meetings in drafty school halls and Guide huts, or camp out on some threatened heath land or allotment. From there you can distribute bulletin sheets photocopied on eye-catching green or pink A4.

Here is an example of how to address a typical meeting:

> **Since our last AGM I couldn't help noticing that we are four down, making the overall attendance a total of two. This did mean that we were unable to vote for or against the motion of whether or not to picket the swimming pool on its shower curtain policy**

> **Our General Secretary has three times claimed to have made the flapjacks but forgotten to bring them. If there is a problem here we would welcome open discussion but people should not make promises they can't keep.**

> **Lastly, there has been a reported siting of a turd floating in the aforementioned swimming pool. Do members agree that it is our duty to bring such things to the attention of the council, however small?**

WARNING

Community activities can become very boring, especially if you meet someone really interesting. Make sure you can drop the whole thing at a moment's notice.

DO YOU NEED THERAPY?

Do you need therapy? From time to time you have probably asked yourself this question. A particularly painful depression may have prompted you to think about it, or perhaps your friends have been trying to help you towards a realisation by putting psychiatrists' calling cards through your door.

Hanging over you is the suspicion that there might be something wrong with you, and that this might be the reason for your sudden shifts of mood, your anxieties and self doubts. But do you really want the undivided attention of a psychiatrist or would you not prefer to just stay in bed for a while and be visited by friends with flowers?

Unless you go to a psychiatrist you may never know whether there is really something wrong with you. Besides, even if you're perfectly happy, that is no reason not to go to a psychiatrist. You might discover a new neurosis which will make you more interesting to others and enrich your life. Certainly, no psychiatrist will refuse to treat you simply because there's nothing wrong with you.

Choosing Your Therapist

If you've made up your mind to go ahead, there are still more decisions to be made. When it comes to psychotherapy there are a bewildering variety of schools of thought to choose from – Freudian, Jungian, Kleinian and Behaviourist are only a few.

Like me, you may want to shop around and find yourself a 'combination analyst'. The advantage of a Jungian/Freudian or a Freudian/Kleinian/Behaviourist is that if you are not satisfied with their analysis you can ask for a different one in mid-session. For example:

> *Psych.:* The reason you feel so guilty is that you're trying to punish your mother and win the approval of your father.
> *Helen:* What would Jung say about it?
> *Psych.:* Oh well, Jung would say you were trying to punish your father and win the approval of your mother.
> *Helen:* What about Freud?
> *Psych.:* That you and your mother wanted to have sex with your brother.
> *Helen:* Pavlov?

Transference

Under analysis you may well find that your therapist begins to take on the role of a member of your family in your mind – a father figure, or a mother substitute. I have several times been caught out by asking my psychiatrist if I can borrow the car for the evening.

You may also find that as your sessions progress your own symptoms may transfer themselves onto your therapist. As you begin to feel happier and more lighthearted your therapist will become more irritable and tense. What is happening here is that you are driving your therapist mad and it may be a good idea to stop the sessions and find another one.

Group Therapy

As an alternative to seeing a psychiatrist, you might consider group therapy. It is more economical and you may feel the need to work out your problems with others.

Don't forget that you will probably be called on to act out a traumatic scene from someone else's childhood in front of the whole group. I once had to enact the role of someone's pet hamster who died tragically of a heart attack. My performance triggered off some very frightening behaviour in that group member.

You will also be required to enact a traumatic scene from your own experience. Refusal to do so will mean that you are 'holding back from the group' and giving 'negative signals'. You might find that you spend a lot of time sitting quietly at the back, hoping that you don't get picked.

Your counsellor may suggest that you enact your trauma with inanimate objects, rather than group members. This requires great concentration and self control, and you may not instantly warm to the task. I have had to respond to a cushion that was giving me conflicting messages about our relationship and reason with a chair that was being too possessive.

Breaking Down Barriers

Much of the group's attention will focus on the problem of breaking down the barriers which exist between people. After an open exchange of views you will probably be asked to explore each other further with the sensation of touch. If you have been particularly honest about your feelings for other members you may have to suffer the occasional pinch and scratch – I suggest you take this philosophically.

Sometimes a group member will bring your attention to a problem that you were not aware of. Once you are aware of it you may wish that you weren't. When one of our group decided to take off all his clothes, some of us felt that we would have preferred him to keep them on, in spite of the barrier he felt this was creating between himself and us.

The whole cathartic experience of group therapy should radically alter the way you think and relate. You will find that relationships within the group will change dramatically throughout the therapy. During one session our group sustained a broken ankle, a stroke, a divorce, a birth and a fractured rib. If you find the experience too overwhelming you may feel the need to explain that you wish to support the group from a non-participatory point of view, and leave quietly.

Self Help

When it comes to your mental health, it's as well not to underestimate your own power to heal yourself. I employ a variety of therapeutic exercises to relieve stress and restore my mental balance. These include: 'Going on holiday therapy', 'Eating a large meal therapy' and 'Spending a lot of money in a shop therapy'. Support from a colleague in any or all of these activities is always helpful.

Co-counselling. This can be mutually beneficial and provide a necessary release of emotions. I release my emotions every Friday with a particularly stimulating counsellor I met at my neighbourhood advice centre.

HOLIDAYS

If you've decided that a holiday will do you good, you will naturally be concerned to make the most of your precious time. Although a thousand things can go wrong, some of them *can* be anticipated. It's not easy to make exactly the right choices, so here is some practical advice gleaned from my own experience.

Choosing a Companion

Going on holiday puts an unnatural strain on a relationship. Any potential holiday companion should be subjected to a rigorous examination as people's behaviour can change drastically once they know that they are on holiday. You may not feel properly prepared when your sensitive and accommodating companion suddenly produces a can of Red Stripe and starts singing, 'Here we go, here we go' on the plane.

Make sure that you and your partner have similar interests and expect the same thing from your holiday. If you are intent on sunbathing for two weeks you will not benefit from a companion who only wants to visit Byzantine churches. Any compromise that you might arrive at will be unsatisfactory, possibly leaving you with a tan in the shape of a church window.

On the other hand, a companion who has no strong feelings and is too eager to go along with whatever you want may also turn out to be a burden.

> *Helen:* What do you want to do?
> *Companion:* I don't mind, what do you want to do?

Helen:	I only want to do what you want to do.
Companion:	I only want to do what *you* want to do.
Helen:	I only want to do what you want to do if you want to do it.
Companion:	I only want to do what you want to do, if you want to do it, but not if you're doing it just because you think I want to do it.

After three days at the airport, we compromised and went home.

To avoid all these hazards, you may prefer to travel on your own. You can, at your own pace, wander around galleries and museums and miss out the most important paintings and statues without anyone ever checking up on you. If you start to feel lonely, simply wave a coloured hanky above your head. You will soon attract a posse of keen tourists in plastic rain hats, who will listen attentively to whatever you have to say and reward you with some foreign coins when you leave.

Overland Trekking in Rugged Terrain

Contrary to expectations you will not meet hardy adventurers and pioneering explorers, but frightened homesick teachers from Coventry who have forgotten their insect repellant. You will, however, have plenty of time to get to know them.

Only go on an overland trek if you feel confident about changing your clothes in the back of a Landrover, and remember: there are ways of being popular in a group without offering sexual favours.

The Backwaters and Riverways of Southern France

If you are canoeing in the Dordogne, do not carry your

passport, money, travellers cheques and clean clothes unless you are familiar with the rapids.

If you want to remain inconspicuous in a French rural village, wear a Gallic peasant hat and a faded Breton stripey shirt, this will make you indistinguishable from all the other British tourists.

Caravan Holidays

It might not be too late for you to cancel your caravan holiday. If you rush. Don't blame yourself, it's a mistake anyone could make.

Camping in the Lake District

1. If you must go camping in the Lakes, don't rush out of your tent in the middle of the night to the toilet in a howling gale if you suffer from back trouble

2. Do not allow sub-zero temperatures to tempt you to light your primus stove inside your tent.

Getting Away from It All on an Island Paradise

I once marooned myself on a deserted beach where I could only see one other person for miles of uninterrupted sand. Unfortunately, he turned out to be a pickpocket.

Package Holidays in Spain

Watch out for tourists who wade into the sea and come out after only fifteen seconds, claiming that it's too cold. It may be that they've decided it is just too far to walk to the municipal WC.

Once you have found your space on the beach, your suntan lotion will be confiscated and then hired back to you.

At six thousand pesetas you may think that the deck chair you are sitting in is yours to take home as a souvenir. This is not the case.

Spanish Jails

Very similar to package holidays but more fun with more interesting companions.

LIVING WITH YOURSELF

One Sunday morning you may wake up alone, and have to face the prospect of the whole day sprawling ahead of you with nothing to do. Like so many others in this situation, you may end up filling it with a particularly slow cup of coffee in the British Museum or leaving rambling messages on all your friends' answering machines.

Classified Ads

A look through the back pages of your Sunday paper may throw up a few possibilities. Without ever moving from your seat you can book a course of aromatherapy, agree to look after someone's cat, time share a cottage in Wales, order three copies of *I Can and I Will* and arrange to be a live-in baby-sitter in a non-smoking vegetarian household even though you don't want to move.

But how can you put meaning into days like this which seem to have been designated void and formless? Looking around your living space you will notice the unmistakable signs of self neglect. A pile of black dustbin bags in the corner of your bedroom are full of clothes to be sorted out at some future date. A cardboard filing system and some sticky labels are still in the bag in which you bought them from Rymans in 1976. A cursory glance under the sink will reveal a discouraging tangle of brillo pads, turpentine and picture wire.

Suddenly you are visited by inspiration. You will completely reorganise your life!

Your Organisation Programme

A new and positive attitude to your surroundings will complement your new resolution. Instead of being in a complete mess, your belongings are now in a state of mid-organisation. From the corner shop you will procure a fresh set of dustbin bags in which to place your old dustbin bags under the new categories 'to be sorted out now', 'to be sorted out later', 'to be ironed and then sorted out'. At any given moment you are able to assess your dustbin bag situation at a glance.

Your now critical eye will see disorder everywhere. You will start to move your furniture half an inch to the right so that it lines up with your pictures, then move it half an inch to the left so that it lines up with your rug. Your books, randomly stacked on shelves, are badly in need of a comprehensive system of categorisation. But which system to choose? After much consideration you decide to group them under 'Authors who are bald', 'Authors who wear glasses' and 'Authors who wear polo necks'.

You are now primed up and ready to attack the major organisational task of the day – your personal documents, bank statements, letters and photographs. A hundred new categories leap into your head. 'Things to be thrown out', 'Things to be kept', 'Things that I don't want to throw out now, because they might be useful later', 'Things to be thrown out in three months' time if they still haven't turned out to be useful'.

Letters and Photographs

The discovery of old letters and photographs may bring your organisational programme to a grinding halt. Your resolutions will melt away and you will be lost in a three-hour reverie, crying over love letters and gazing mournfully at photographs of your younger self. Tearfully you will ask yourself the question why you can't be as happy now as you were then – or why you can't be as unhappy now as you were then.

To save the day you must find some way of accommodating these feelings into your overall strategy. With a fresh pile of dustbin bags, file your letters and photographs under the general heading of 'Depths of emotion felt'. Your new system will contain letters and photographs under the categories 'Regret felt', 'Remorse felt', 'Guilt at lack of remorse felt', 'Misery', 'Desperate misery' and 'Suicidal misery'.

At the end of the day, with a certain sense of achievement, you may take a break and survey the day's work. Stepping over the rows of dustbin bags which line the floor, you may marvel that the sum total of your possessions seems to have doubled or even tripled since you began.

LOOKING AFTER YOUR MONEY

Reading Your Bank Statement

Examining your bank statement can raise some interesting questions. How is it that I managed to spend £300 on 7 March when I didn't even leave the house that day? And how did I manage to spend £259 at John Lewis when I only spent three minutes in there sheltering from the rain? I have often suspected that there is someone possibly in a parallel universe who is spending the money in my account.

Unfortunately my bank manager is unnecessarily sceptical about paranormal phenomena and has been known to write me some hurtful letters. On these occasions a well-crafted reply is called for:

> Dear Bank Manager,
>
> I know from your last letter that you feel I have not yet realised my growth potential and that you find it difficult to justify my expenditure in the following areas:
>
> Honey from Wales £37.50
>
> Jumper £88 (it was reduced from £98 so that's really a saving of £10)
>
> Standing order to three magazines

These items are in fact essential to my development and will eventually benefit me financially in a way in which I would dearly like to come in and discuss with you. Unfortunately I'm going away to Paris for six weeks which is one of the reasons I am writing to you.

You may wonder why Paris? Well may I say that there is a slim, if not almost definite chance that I might be in a position to earn some money or at least make contacts when I am over there.

In order to allay your fears I enclose a list of how I am going to economise while away: I will limit myself to three croissants a day, and I will often exclaim 'Trop chère' very loudly in supermarkets.

Yours,

Helen

If even such a letter fails to persuade him to keep your bank account open you may, like me, have to withdraw your custom and organise your own finances. I start off by taking a firm line:

Dear Helen,
I am very disappointed in your spendthrift attitude and I must warn you that you will be in deep trouble if you go on spending money at this rate.

Yours,

Helen

If I ignore this a second letter usually arrives:

> **Dear Helen,**
> It has now been two weeks since my last letter and you have clearly made no attempt to economise. Failure to cut back on your spending will force me to take drastic measures.
>
> **Yours,**
>
> **Helen**

If I still don't take any notice I get very stern and confiscate my own cheque card, which doesn't really make any difference because it's two years out of date anyway.

Choosing banks: *Choose your bank carefully and it could save you a lot of time and embarrassment. I can give this advice because I have surveyed not only the high street banks but also most foreign banks with branches within eighty miles of my home. Allied Channel Islands is a winner – courteous service, few questions asked and some very helpful staff.*

INSTANT
DINNER PARTIES

When a group of hungry revellers turns up unexpectedly on your doorstep there is no need to panic. The essence of coping is making the most of your resources. This is a meal which I rustled up in under two minutes. It's amazing what you can do with two Weetabix, a jar of Marmite and a tube of tomato paste.

Nouvelle cuisine.

Weetabix sorbet

*Marmite surprise
with grated Weetabix*

*Weetabix bake
with Legumes
of Weetabix*

Weetabix Benedict.

BEING LATE

When you're in a hurry to leave the house or you have to be somewhere important at short notice there are a number of strategies that can save you precious minutes.

1. Always keep a change of clothes under your pillow to save on ironing.
2. While running your bath, fill your coffee mug from the hot tap.
3. If there's no time for a bath, spray air-freshner on localised areas of your clothes.
4. A Weetabix sandwich eaten on the bus can provide a balanced breakfast.
5. Invest in a child's plastic beaker to prevent tea spilling while going round corners.

Making a Dash

Just because you're in a hurry there's no need to lose your sense of style. Outfits can be thrown together in a matter of seconds and yet create a sophisticated and elegant impression.

A CONFESSION

I have taken you now quite some distance along the road to coping with your life, but I feel it is time for me to make a disclosure of a very personal nature.

I have often admired the courageous example of people in the Arts who are prepared to share with their public a private affliction. The number of National Theatre players who felt able to go public about their dyslexia after Susan Hampshire's noble disclosure was magnificent.

I myself would have willingly joined their ranks had I been able to claim this particular disability. Though as it happens, and as any of my teachers will testify, my hand-writing and spelling at Blackheath High School were commended on several occasions, being described as 'excellent' by one teacher and 'very neat' by another.

It is a tribute to human nature that all this publicity didn't damage Miss Hampshire's career. In fact shortly afterwards Susan starred in a long running West End play.

If I therefore take this opportunity to make my own revelations it is only in the hope that I may, in some small way, help others who are also suffering quietly and alone. If it also results in the offer of a West End role, so be it.

My confession is: I haven't got a perfectly tidy airing cupboard with beautifully folded towels filed in order of size and colour. Also, when I was thirteen I stole clothes for my Cindy doll and then lied about it when questioned.

This condition is known as Afalaxia. Perhaps one day I might be the patron of a society or pressure group or maybe front a drama documentary on the subject.

SOCIAL SKILLS

Not all of us can be plumbers or mechanics. Getting things done means communicating with people who have skills which are different to your own. You can easily get on with people from most professions by following the prescribed conversational rules.

Visiting gas men, plumbers, carpenters: *Stick to tea and the weather – 'Hot enough for you', 'Bitter out' etc*

Hairdressers: *preferred subject is 'holidays'. If you haven't been on one, talk about where you'd like to go or simply pretend you've been to Spain*

Taxi drivers: *anything will do here, as the glass partition rarely lets through any discernible sound. However, this shouldn't prevent you establishing a firm rapport. The fact that you can't hear each other is all for the best*

Mechanics: *try to be sympathetic and see it from their point of view:*

> 'I wonder if you could possibly see your way to having a bit of a look at the car ... the Renault yes, you might have noticed it in your yard ... it's been there for a few weeks, actually. But there again, I'm sure there are a lot of cars in your garage that are far more worthy of your attention than mine, but if you could just give me some sort of indication as to roughly when the car might perhaps at least have been looked at, I'm not talking about anything as definite or specific as a date. Nothing as inflexible as that! But if you feel it might be

say, a next September sort of date as opposed to a next May sort of a date, perhaps you could just give me a sign, maybe nod your head – a cough or a even a sigh would be helpful.'

BEING
A HOUSE GUEST

When you are invited to stay at a friend's it is best not to take everything you are told at face value – as I discovered to my cost. 'What's mine is yours' does not mean you can slip a marble egg into your bag if it takes your fancy. 'Help yourself to anything in the kitchen' means only accept food at meal times or when offered. I badly offended a host once when I 'made myself feel at home' by breaking things and padding about naked. In other people's houses a code of behaviour has to be observed.

Here is how I dealt with a potentially awkward situation in the bathroom:

Helen: Oh, Jean, yes . . . er . . . slight shortage in the papyrus department . . .

Jean: In the cupboard on the landing.

Helen: I'd sooner stay put if it's all the same to you.

Jean: Perhaps you'd like something to read? I'll pop something under the door shall I? The *Observer* supplement do?

Helen: Fine.

Here, as you can see, I managed to communicate my needs yet maintain my dignity.

The bathroom can of course be the source of much

embarrassment. This is largely due to the unpredictability of other people's plumbing. I have often agonised late at night over whether to pull the chain and risk waking the entire house or set the alarm for six o'clock in the morning and finish off before anyone wakes up. One alternative is to carry some adhesive tape and a sticker 'This lavatory is out of order'.

A more permanent solution is to check on the flushing mechanism in advance. I make a point of taking a quick look at the ballcock of any house I am visiting for the first time. A trial flush can avoid much embarrassment later. I enter the details in my diary for later reference so that I can be prepared on a return visit:

Description: *Victorian porcelain*

Noise level: *High*

Rate of refill: *Thirty-two minutes*

Side effects on rest of plumbing: *Extensive radiator rattle, sink gurgle in kitchen*

Observations: *a slow starter but powerful flush – can be temperamental, needs up to three attempts. Responds to surprise flush. Approach casually, looking in other direction then suddenly turn and flush*

Sometimes, even after these precautions, discretion is impossible. If you are defeated by a determinedly loud toilet, which shouts to the whole household 'Someone's just been to the lavvy!' summon your fellow guests into the room and announce confidently that you are about to visit the lavatory.

CAKES

A Special Cake For a Special Occasion

Nothing shows you care more for a person than baking them a surprise cake. Never mind if there isn't a birthday or wedding – pick any occasion. Surprise is the essence. Just think of something personal about a loved one and then sculpt it in sponge!

Here is a cake I made for someone who came round in tears because her period was late. Wasting no time I set to in the kitchen. I came up with this little gem to cheer her up.

GUILT

In spite of yourself, you might sometimes have dangerous fantasies that make you feel deeply ashamed. It is important that you learn to see these fantasies for what they are and not allow yourself to be undermined by them. Like me you ought to be able to accept and acknowledge them.

My Fantasy

I occasionally fantasise that I am Jane Asher for the day in a pine kitchen with perfect children and a wonderful husband. Fortunately I have learnt how to cope with this fantasy.

Living with Guilt

The subconscious mind sometimes throws up disturbing images which go against everything you believe in or are trying to achieve. You may feel extremely guilty, particularly if those feelings concern your fellow sex and are hostile.

While struggling with this issue my attention was drawn to an ad in my local paper for a seminar weekend entitled 'Feminism and Fancy Underwear: Can they be reconciled?' Wasting no time I jumped on the next train.

Friday evening was spent mapping out who would attend which lectures. On Saturday afternoon we divided into separate factions discussing fabrics, separates and hoserie respectively. We then decamped to picket the hoserie department at Debenhams. I ended up buying an attractive tartan overnight bag and a headscarf. I later discovered the weekend had been infiltrated by the local Women's Institute which made any findings redundant.

COPING
WITH CHRISTMAS

It's a sad fact that for many of us Christmas is a traumatic time, full of emotional upsets, when we feel compelled to drink too much, overeat and say things that we later regret. I have found that by behaving in this way throughout the year Christmas is far more tolerable, passing by just like any other day.

A Time For Giving

Being properly prepared for Christmas means that you will have spent months in the kitchen selflessly baking cakes and making nativity scenes. You will also have paid attention to passing references and hints made by friends and relatives throughout the year and will be able to provide them with just the right gift when they arrive at your home.

Last Minute Planning

If, however, you have failed in one or possibly even all of these respects, have not bought anything for anyone and are therefore considering emigration/suicide, it is important not to panic. You must make some realistic estimations of what you can do in the time you have left – even if it's only a few seconds.

Panic Buying

Panic buying won't help. It's no use recklessly buying anything out of desperation just because the shops are open. My cupboards are, at this moment, full of several hundredweight of tins of cat meat and three years' worth of 'Snugglers' which are no good to me or anyone else.

Making Presents in Under Five Minutes

People like to receive something that you've put a little thought into, even made yourself, and no one is to know whether the thought took you just three seconds. A pair of scissors and a strip of masking tape can work miracles. I have given many last-minute presents in my time and only offended a few close friends in the process.

Start by taking stock of what you already have lying about the house and see if you can't adapt it into presents. With a little imagination an old Hoover bag can become a slipper bag for spare shoes, a lavatory brush can become a doll for a child, an old formica tray might be very decorative with a few pictures from magazines stuck on it, or perhaps you have something from an abandoned evening class that someone would be very proud to receive?

If you're really stuck for something to wrap up, why not use the scissors to square up the wrapping paper itself and give it as a poster?

Themes

If you have difficulty coming up with new ideas for presents, it's a good idea to establish a theme which you can add to each year. One Christmas I bought a nephew a bottle of ink, the next year a nib and the next a pen. One year my theme was that all my presents were late, the next that none of them turned up at all.

Time and Imagination

If you have more time and can knit, the choice of presents is, almost limitless. This knitted answering machine cover is a handy present idea that I had myself and anyone would be delighted to receive. You could apply the same principle to any object in a friend or relative's possession. Look around, they must have a food mixer, a television or a lampshade that hasn't yet been covered.

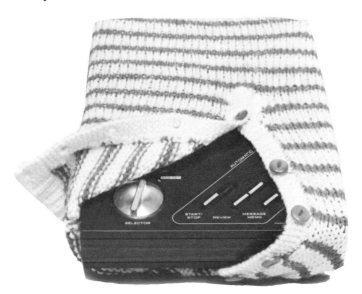

Receiving Presents

Sometimes instead of a present you may receive a card saying that the money for your present has been donated to charity. I am always touched by this gesture and almost prefer it to receiving a gift. However, I do feel it necessary to write back and ask for a chit from the charity concerned confirming that a donation has been received.

Thank You Letters

Thank you letters are an opportunity to keep in contact with relatives you rarely see:

Dear Aunt Evelyn,

Thank you so much for the extremely bright jumper – what a cheerful colour! It certainly has given me an opportunity to extend my wardrobe, which at the moment doesn't contain any turquoise clothes. Perhaps I'll buy some turquoise practice slacks or a lovely winter muff to match! Christmas for us this year was tremendously eventful.

Lots of love as ever,

Helen

Dear Helen,

I was thrilled to learn that you'd decided to help people in need this year and buy all your presents from Oxfam! Though I must admit to being a little bit anxious about what I might receive – a wicker plant holder or a broken fire with a furry flex perhaps? That's why it was such a relief and a delight to receive such a lovely pair of secondhand pants.

Yours,

Aunt Evelyn

Birthdays can be a painful indication of your popularity. I keep an old set of birthday cards in store to swell the numbers. The ones labelled 'Now you are ten' sometimes remind me of happier times when I was a child and people had to turn up to my birthday parties because their mothers brought them.

'People often ask me how I manage to combine a career and a happy and fulfilled social life with being an innovative and tireless human being. Why do people ask me this? Because I lie to them.'